WOMEN OF DESTINY

Ap. Rosemary Duncanson

Copyright © 2024 by Cyril & Dorise Publishing

All rights reserved.

No part of this publication may be reproduced, distributed, or transmitted in any form or by any means, including photocopying, recording, or other electronic or mechanical methods, without the prior written permission of the publisher, except in the case of brief quotations embodied in critical reviews and certain other non-commercial uses permitted by copyright law.

For permission requests, write to the publisher, addressed "Attention:

Permissions Coordinator," at the address below.

Harmony Close,

Kewtown,

Providenciales

Turks & Caicos Islands

ISBN: 9781739369194

https://www.cyrilanddorsiepublishing.com/

CONTENTS

CHAPTER 1 WOMEN OF DESTINY 1

CHAPTER 2 GOD CHOOSES WHOM HE MAY 10

CHAPTER 3 BE THE MESSENGER 12

CHAPTER 4 LET ME SPEAK! 16

CHAPTER 5 THE APOSTLE 18

CHAPTER 6 THE VOICE OF THE PROPHETS
LET ME SPEAK! 19

CHAPTER 7 THE VOICE OF THE PROPHETS
GOD CALLS ORDINARY PEOPLE TO DO
EXTRAORDINARY THINGS 22

CHAPTER 8 PROPHETESS MIRIAM 24

CHAPTER 9 SARAH SPEAKS THE MOTHER OF
NATIONS 25

CHAPTER 10 PROPHETESS HANNAH
THE PRAYER WARRIOR 26

CHAPTER 11 ABIGAIL
THE PROPHETESS WITH GREAT WISDOM 29

CHAPTER 12 HULDAH
THE JUDGEMENT PROPHETESS 31

CHAPTER 13 THE SPIRIT OF THE EVANGELIST 34

CHAPTER 14 COME SEE A MAN 36

CHAPTER 15 THE PASTOR
PHEBE GOD'S FAITHFUL SERVANT 37

CHAPTER 16 THE TEACHER
AQUILA AND PRISCILLA 39

CHAPTER 17 LET THE WORD OF GOD SPEAK FOR
ITSELF 41

CHAPTER 18 WOMAN OF FAITH THE
SYROPHOENICIAN WOMAN 43

CHAPTER 19 WOMAN OF FAITH
ONE TOUCH 46

CHAPTER 20 THE VIRTUOUS WOMAN
WOMAN OF PROMINENCE 48

ABOUT THE AUTHOR 51

LETTERS TO GOD 52

CHAPTER 1
WOMEN OF DESTINY

Today, many women from all spheres of life are still confused and have been beaten up and rejected by some male pastors who have forbidden women to preach in the church. This concept has led many down the road to destruction, crippling and stagnating them from coming forward. The enemy knows that if we stay blindfolded by these deceptive lies, not only will it kill our ministries, but it will have a great effect on those who do not know the truth.

We must understand if we are going to win the many fights that the enemy is sending our way in these last days, we must be equipped to fight back by any means. Being or keeping silent in the church is never a good way to fight the enemy if we are going to win the war. We must realize that the enemy doesn't care who he uses, as long as he wins. Our determination must be one of a strong courage and a made up mind no matter what happens.

Isaiah 41:10

Fear thou not; for I am with thee: be not dismayed; for I am thy God: I will strengthen thee; yea, I will help thee; yea, I will uphold thee with the right hand of my righteousness.

One of the many scriptures that most unbelievers of women preachers teach, is found in the book of 1Corinthians 14:34-35:

> *34 Let your women keep silence in the churches: for it is not permitted unto them to speak; but they are commanded to be under obedience as also saith the law.*
>
> *35 And if they will learn any thing, let them ask their husbands at home: for it is a shame for women to speak in the church.*

Many male preachers have often used this scripture to justify themselves rejecting women to preach or teach the Word of God in the church. Friends, we can never use one or two scriptures from the Word of God to justify our way of thinking. We should search the scriptures and study the Word of God so that we can become a productive testament of God's truth.

Let us kindly go back to 1Corinthians chapter 14 and start at the very beginning. It quotes, *"Follow after charity, and desire spiritual gifts, but rather that ye may prophesy."* Look at verse two closely, *"For he that speaketh in an unknown tongue speaketh not unto men, but unto God: for no man understandeth him; howbeit in the spirit he speaketh mysteries."*

Furthermore, let's also examine 1Corinthians 14:3, *"But he that prophesieth speaketh unto men to edification, and exhortation, and comfort."* Here the Apostle Paul is making a good illustration of God's word to the church. One is unable to comprehend what he or she speaks, without the interpretation all mysteries belongs to God; without the power of the Holy Ghost been made known to men, it is highly impossible to understand this. In verses *3, 4* and *6*, the Apostle Paul is making it clear that it is of not much use to be speaking in an unknown tongue if the church does not understand. In verse 5, Apostle Paul is stating that he prefers if one prophesies than speak with tongues because prophecy with understanding edifies the church. When the church is edified, it brings clarity and consolation. In verses *7,8,9* and *10* the Apostle Paul is making it clear that there must be a distinction in sounds as well as voices. According to verse *11* you and I won't be able to understand each other's language when it is of no use to each of us. Here the Apostle Paul makes it clear enough that tongues must be interpreted if they are to be effective. If we continue to look closely at scripture, we see that from verses *20* to *24* of this same text that tongues are a sign to the unbelievers. Apostle Paul is encouraging the church to become mature. Verse *22* makes it very clear and states, *"Wherefore tongues are for a sign, not to them that believe, but to them that believe not: but prophesying serveth not for them that believe not, but for them which believe."*

We must be willing to search the scriptures and be able to understand, if we want to win the battles for our minds. In verses *26* to *40*, the Apostle Paul is bringing order in the church. If you and I are going to become mature, we must be able to adapt to the principles of God's Word. Let us look closely at verses *34* and *39*. In verse *34*, the Apostle Paul is forbidding the women to speak as pertaining to the law. Here it is very clear that such confusion to speak publicly was not tolerated, such is as the transgression of Eve. Now take a close look at verse *39*, it is clear that the Apostle Paul's message was to set order in the church that was among unruly believers who were under the law at that time and were causing confusion and havoc in the church with each other. We must not allow someone's misconduct and their evil ways of thinking to silence the many prophetic voices, be it males or females. In the Earth we must be moved by grace, for by it, we are saved through faith. It's our gift from God, He wants us to speak of it, we can never be silenced about it.

Ephesians 2:8-9

8 For by grace are ye saved through faith; and that not of yourselves: it is the gift of God:

9 Not of works, lest any man should boast.

We must understand that we are no longer prisoners and slaves to some man-made laws. God freed us, He paid a price we could not pay. We owed a debt we could not pay, He made himself a ransom for mankind by dying on the cross and redeeming us back to Him through His precious blood.

Hebrews 9:22-28

22 And almost all things are by the law purged with blood; and without shedding of blood is no remission.

23 It was therefore necessary that the patterns of things in the heavens should be purified with these; but the heavenly things themselves with better sacrifices than these.

24 For Christ is not entered into the holy places made with hands, which are the figures of the true; but into heaven itself, now to appear in the presence of God for us:

25 Nor yet that he should offer himself often, as the high priest entereth into the holy place every year with blood of others;

26 For then must he often have suffered since the foundation of the world: but now once in the end of the world hath he appeared to put away sin by the sacrifice of himself.

27 And as it is appointed unto men once to die, but after this the judgment:

28 So Christ was once offered to bear the sins of many; and unto them that look for him shall he appear the second time without sin unto salvation.

We must be willing to stand up and fight the enemy back with every fibre of our being, and be ready to become a witness and a testament of that truth. In order to do so, we must become that witness calling darkness into light. If we are going to be that candlestick, we can never be silent.

Let me take you back to 1Corinthains11, verses *3,4* and *13*. The Apostle Paul stated that every woman praying or prophesying must cover her head, he did not deny her from speaking, furthermore they were to judge in themselves for the woman is not without the man, neither is the man without the woman. If we should take it a little further in 1Timothy 2:8-14 the Apostle Paul made it clear here:

> *I will therefore that men pray every where, lifting up holy hands, without wrath and doubting.*
>
> *9 In like manner also, that women adorn themselves in modest apparel, with shamefacedness and sobriety; not with broided hair, or gold, or pearls, or costly array;*
>
> *10 But (which becometh women professing godliness) with good works.*
>
> *11 Let the woman learn in silence with all subjection.*
>
> *12 But I suffer not a woman to teach, nor to usurp authority over the man, but to be in silence.*
>
> *13 For Adam was first formed, then Eve.*
>
> *14 And Adam was not deceived, but the woman being deceived was in the transgression.*

Friends it is clear that the Apostle Paul was peaking clearly to a woman in relation to her husband, that she be in subjection to him, she was not to teach or usurp his authority and therefore made mention of Adam and Eve. There is nothing here to prove that a woman shouldn't preach, teach or speak in the church. Many false teachers have made many voices to become silent by some scriptures they themselves do not understand and have used these rebellious acts of these unruly women, making many others a victim of past events that took place under the law. However, they fail to comprehend the finish work of the cross and if we ought to take it a little further, consider the pouring out of the Holy Spirit according to Joel 2:28:

> "**28** *And it shall come to pass afterward, that I will pour out my spirit upon all flesh; and your sons and your daughters shall prophesy, your old men shall dream dreams, your young men shall see visions:*"

Friends, let's not be naive here; this is a wonderful promise concerning you and me, our Lord never placed any limits on His children, His promise is to all flesh by pouring out his spirit upon them all. If we ought to experience such refreshing, we can never be a silent church. Proclaiming the good news of the kingdom brings the blessings of God. We must be able to rise up and kill all religious spirits that keep us from becoming all that God has created us to be.

Many women have been prisoners in their minds, believing that they must just sit and be silent, but that is not the will of God for them. For many years they have believed this fairytale, many refuse to participate in women's conferences and other church activities that involve public speaking. Refusing the pulpit due to this misleading teaching, their ministries can never be birthed, lest being the spiritual leaders that God has called them to become. Such strongholds of the enemy left many of them in a stagnated place for many years. While many are coming out of their prison houses, many are crippled by this deceptive lie. Today I am encouraging women from all walks of life to rise up and be the voice in the midst of the darkness, for many are dying spiritually and losing many battles refusing to become that voice in the Earth. Friends, there is no such thing as sitting silently. You have been anointed to call darkness into light. The enemy knows that if only your eyes can become open, he is in trouble. Many "so-called" preachers that refuse to see the truth in God's Word allowed such belief to stop the many voices of God in the Earth. Joel chapter 2 made it very clear, verse 25 of that chapter states, *"And I will restore to you the years that the locust hath eaten, the cankerworm, and the caterpiller, and the palmerworm, my great army which I sent among you."* Friends I have no doubt that restoration is here, we are that army, a force to be reckoned with, the enemy knows that he is in trouble. It is time to take that stand and be the voice on the mountain top.

CHAPTER 2
GOD CHOOSES WHOM HE MAY

Galatians 3: 28-29

28 There is neither Jew nor Greek, there is neither bond nor free, there is neither male nor female: for ye are all one in Christ Jesus.

29 And if ye be Christ's, then are ye Abraham's seed, and heirs according to the promise.

Friends, here again the Apostle Paul is speaking to the church of Galatia making it very clear that there is no differentiation between male or female, Jew or Greek, free or bound with God, for we are all one in Him. Here we must be of understanding that when we stand before God to give an account of the things done on planet Earth, no one will be responsible for what you and I have done. Our spouses won't be able to answer to God for us, yet we sometimes deceive ourselves believing that we are responsible for each other. Rest assured that you and you alone will stand before the judgement-seat to answer for yourself. There won't be any spouses there, we must stop letting the enemy trick us by using the many bad seeds he has sown in our minds to believe such fairytales. It is very important that we search the scriptures for ourselves so that we can be that voice that God is calling us to be.

CHAPTER 3
BE THE MESSENGER

Matthew 28-1:8

In the end of the sabbath, as it began to dawn toward the first day of the week, came Mary Magdalene and the other Mary to see the sepulchre.

2 And, behold, there was a great earthquake: for the angel of the Lord descended from heaven, and came and rolled back the stone from the door, and sat upon it.

3 His countenance was like lightning, and his raiment white as snow:

4 And for fear of him the keepers did shake, and became as dead men.

5 And the angel answered and said unto the women, Fear not ye: for I know that ye seek Jesus, which was crucified.

6 He is not here: for he is risen, as he said. Come, see the place where the Lord lay.

7 And go quickly, and tell his disciples that he is risen from the dead; and, behold, he goeth before you into Galilee; there shall ye see him: lo, I have told you.

8 And they departed quickly from the sepulchre with fear and great joy; and did run to bring his disciples word.

This is one of the most profound stories in the Bible that pertained to these particular two Marys in scripture. These two women had such great encounters with Jesus. Mary Magdalene, who was one of His followers, was a witness to His crucifixion and resurrection. It was Mary who anointed the feet of Jesus, accompanied by Mary the mother of James and Salome who went to the tomb to anoint the body of Jesus.

Matthew 28-5:9

And the angel answered and said unto the women, Fear not ye: for I know that ye seek Jesus, which was crucified.

6 He is not here: for he is risen, as he said. Come, see the place where the Lord lay.

7 And go quickly, and tell his disciples that he is risen from the dead; and, behold, he goeth before you into Galilee; there shall ye see him: lo, I have told you.

8 And they departed quickly from the sepulchre with fear and great joy; and did run to bring his disciples word.

9 And as they went to tell his disciples, behold, Jesus met them, saying, All hail. And they came and held him by the feet, and worshipped him.

Friends the fact that is so interesting about this is their loyalty and worship to God, after all they were His messengers of that true light, we don't have to argue the fact that worship is within; out of the mouth speaks what's in the heart.

Luke 6:45

A good man out of the good treasure of his heart bringeth forth that which is good; and an evil man out of the evil treasure of his heart bringeth forth that which is evil: for of the abundance of the heart his mouth speaketh.

Friends, we must be willing to tell others about the goodness of God in order to bring them to Him. If we cannot speak of his goodness, we won't become effective ambassadors of the kingdom for Him. These women were real worshippers of Christ, nothing or no one could have silenced them from demonstrating authentic worship.

CHAPTER 4
LET ME SPEAK!

Ephesians 4:11-16

11 And he gave some, apostles; and some, prophets; and some, evangelists; and some, pastors and teachers;

12 For the perfecting of the saints, for the work of the ministry, for the edifying of the body of Christ:

13 Till we all come in the unity of the faith, and of the knowledge of the Son of God, unto a perfect man, unto the measure of the stature of the fulness of Christ:

14 That we henceforth be no more children, tossed to and fro, and carried about with every wind of doctrine, by the sleight of men, and cunning craftiness, whereby they lie in wait to deceive;

15 But speaking the truth in love, may grow up into him in all things, which is the head, even Christ:

16 From whom the whole body fitly joined together and compacted by that which every joint supplieth, according to the effectual working in the measure of

every part, maketh increase of the body unto the edifying of itself in love.

It is of good understanding that the gates of hell will not prevail against the true church of God. For the church has been built upon the Apostles, prophets, and Jesus Himself being the chief cornerstone

Ephesians 2:20-22

20 And are built upon the foundation of the apostles and prophets, Jesus Christ himself being the chief corner stone;

21 In whom all the building fitly framed together groweth unto an holy temple in the Lord:

22 In whom ye also are builded together for an habitation of God through the Spirit.

Yet today, so many have not yet come to the realization that we need each other if we will win this war. No one individual can carry out this great assignment of the church, for she was founded upon its Apostles and prophets, with our Lord as our shield.

CHAPTER 5
THE APOSTLE

Romans 16:7

7 Salute Andronicus and Junia, my kinsmen, and my fellow-prisoners, who are of note among the apostles, who also were in Christ before me.

Here it is clear that Junia was the first woman Apostle in the Bible, despite a good deal of confusion from the theologians. It does not deny the fact that she was named among the Apostles. Apostle Paul had spoken highly of Junia as a prominent Apostle who had been imprisoned for her labour. Today many great Apostles are still being persecuted for their labour of love by promoting the gospel, but like the Apostle Junia even if it should cause our life, we must be willing to go the extra mile for our Lord and Saviour.

CHAPTER 6
THE VOICE OF THE PROPHETS LET ME SPEAK!

Esther 4:16

Go, gather together all the Jews that are present in Shushan, and fast ye for me, and neither eat nor drink three days, night or day: I also and my maidens will fast likewise; and so will I go in unto the king, which is not according to the law: and if I perish, I perish.

Here is a story about a Jewish girl named Esther who didn't give a second thought about standing up for the freedom of her people. Her words in chapter 4 of Esther, verse *16*, speak profoundly of her. She was willing to fast and take a stand to free her people from a wicked decree that had been made by Haman who sought to have all the Jews killed in the Persian Empire. Esther, who had concealed her identity, later went before the king, found favour with him, and became the queen, risking her life; she saved the people from the wicked plot of Haman. From this story, we can see that Esther was not selfish, she was a voice to keep her people alive. Yet, many today want to silence the many voices from coming forth. You must never allow the enemy to silence you. You must be willing to stand up and fight back by whatever means and be that voice that will save your nation.

Ephesians 4:11-16

11 And he gave some, apostles; and some, prophets; and some, evangelists; and some, pastors and teachers;

12 For the perfecting of the saints, for the work of the ministry, for the edifying of the body of Christ:

13 Till we all come in the unity of the faith, and of the knowledge of the Son of God, unto a perfect man, unto the measure of the stature of the fulness of Christ:

14 That we henceforth be no more children, tossed to and fro, and carried about with every wind of doctrine, by the sleight of men, and cunning craftiness, whereby they lie in wait to deceive;

15 But speaking the truth in love, may grow up into him in all things, which is the head, even Christ:

16 From whom the whole body fitly joined together and compacted by that which every joint supplieth, according to the effectual working in the measure of

every part, maketh increase of the body unto the edifying of itself in love.

Here again, the scripture is clear in Ephesians 4 verse 11. Apostle Paul teaches that he gave some Apostle, but it didn't state male or female. The Apostle Paul teaches that there is neither male nor female when pertaining to God. He made it clear we are all one; the purpose of the gifts is to edify and perfect the church until we all become that mature church that God is calling us to become. In order to do so, we must be that voice in the Earth, whether male or female. God anoints whom He wishes.

CHAPTER 7
THE VOICE OF THE PROPHETS GOD CALLS ORDINARY PEOPLE TO DO EXTRAORDINARY THINGS

It is no surprise at all that our Lord called ordinary people to do extraordinary things. Let us take a close look at this scripture found in Luke *1:30:"And the angel said unto her, Fear not, Mary: for thou hast found favour with God."*

Here it is clear that God is no respecter of persons; He choses whom He may. Mary was a commoner, (Joseph was a carpenter), yet God chose her to bring forth the Messiah. We must never underestimate the power of God.

Judges 4:6

And she sent and called Barak the son of Abinoam out of Kedeshnaphtali, and said unto him, Hath not the LORD God of Israel commanded, saying, Go and draw toward mount Tabor, and take with thee ten thousand men of the children of Naphtali and of the children of Zebulun?

Here is the story of a powerful prophetess named Deborah who judged Israel in her day. The biblical teaching of this prophetess and judge help us to understand that we don't have to be trapped by culture, neither by gender. It is God's desire that we, His people, breakthrough from such barriers and pursue after that which He has called us to. You, too, can become a powerful leader and a judge just like prophetess Deborah, fulfilling your divine assignment that you have been called to do. I am convinced your eyes are becoming open, and you are on your way to becoming the mighty warriors that God has predestined since the beginning of time. Let's move on.

CHAPTER 8
PROPHETESS MIRIAM

Exodus 15:20

And Miriam the prophetess, the sister of Aaron, took a timbrel in her hand; and all the women went out after her with timbrels and with dances.

Prophetess Miriam, whose name means *"the God who speaks"* is the first prophetess in the Bible. Her worship and loyalty to God teaches many of today how to lead one into authentic worship. When our worship is sincere before God, there is no telling what God won't do. Here is a prophetess who had done many deeds, from the bravery of delivering her brother Moses to leading the Hebrew women in singing, dancing and playing drums after the crossing of the Red Sea; this made such a great impact with both male and female. This is a reminder that there is no gender, male or female when it comes to God. The voice of the enemy must never speak louder than the voice of God, we must be willing to glorify Him at all times. Never say no when God is saying yes.

CHAPTER 9
SARAH SPEAKS
THE MOTHER OF NATIONS

Genesis 21:10-12

10 Wherefore she said unto Abraham, Cast out this bondwoman and her son: for the son of this bondwoman shall not be heir with my son, even with Isaac.

11 And the thing was very grievous in Abraham's sight because of his son.

12 And God said unto Abraham, Let it not be grievous in thy sight because of the lad, and because of thy bondwoman; in all that Sarah hath said unto thee, hearken unto her voice; for in Isaac shall thy seed be called.

Being remembered as the ancestress of her people, this Prophetess had secured Isaac's position as Abraham's heir. Her name speaks volume as it means *noblewoman* or *Princess Sarai*. Her name had been changed by God, from *my princess,* to Sarah, which now meant *Princess to all*, the ancestress of all nations.

CHAPTER 10
PROPHETESS HANNAH THE PRAYER WARRIOR

1 Samuel 2:1-10

And Hannah prayed, and said, My heart rejoiceth in the LORD, mine horn is exalted in the LORD: my mouth is enlarged over mine enemies; because I rejoice in thy salvation.

2 There is none holy as the LORD: for there is none beside thee: neither is there any rock like our God.

3 Talk no more so exceeding proudly; let not arrogancy come out of your mouth: for the LORD is a God of knowledge, and by him actions are weighed.

4 The bows of the mighty men are broken, and they that stumbled are girded with strength.

5 They that were full have hired out themselves for bread; and they that were hungry ceased: so that the barren hath born seven; and she that hath many children is waxed feeble.

6 The LORD killeth, and maketh alive: he bringeth down to the grave, and bringeth up.

7 The LORD maketh poor, and maketh rich: he bringeth low, and lifteth up.

8 He raiseth up the poor out of the dust, and lifteth up the beggar from the dunghill, to set them among princes, and to make them inherit the throne of glory: for the pillars of the earth are the LORD's, and he hath set the world upon them.

9 He will keep the feet of his saints, and the wicked shall be silent in darkness; for by strength shall no man prevail.

10 The adversaries of the LORD shall be broken to pieces; out of heaven shall he thunder upon them: the LORD shall judge the ends of the earth; and he shall give strength unto his king, and exalt the horn of his anointed.

Serving in the temple of the Lord, Hannah was a devoted and loyal woman who was steadfast in prayer despite her struggles to find self-worth. She later gained victory over her oppressor Peninnah and gave birth to Samuel the prophet. She had been transformed from intense grief to great joy. Her song of deliverance (can be found in 1Samuel 2) is to encourage the church that we should never waver in our faith when putting God to the test. Another powerful truth of this dynamic woman of God is that we should never reap in anger. We should be patient and trust God no matter what the situation is and in due season, we shall reap if we faint not.

CHAPTER 11
ABIGAIL
THE PROPHETESS WITH GREAT WISDOM

1 Samuel 25:32-33

32 And David said to Abigail, Blessed be the LORD God of Israel, which sent thee this day to meet me:

33 And blessed be thy advice, and blessed be thou, which hast kept me this day from coming to shed blood, and from avenging myself with mine own hand.

Here is a wonderful story of a humble and beautiful woman named Abigail who was married to a rich man, called Nabal. Despite Nabal being wealthy, she was faced with a situation where she had to use the wisdom of God. Abigail pleaded with David to save her husband's life and to see things from her perspective so that she and her household could be saved from the approaching enemies toward them by David's orders. We must be able to learn from this great woman of God, that despite our status in society, we must be of a meek and humble spirit. Here she used the wisdom of

God by protecting herself and her household. Humility is the key factor here, letting us know that God resists the proud but will give grace to the humble.

CHAPTER 12
HULDAH
THE JUDGEMENT PROPHETESS

2 Kings 22:13-20

13 Go ye, enquire of the LORD for me, and for the people, and for all Judah, concerning the words of this book that is found: for great is the wrath of the LORD that is kindled against us, because our fathers have not hearkened unto the words of this book, to do according unto all that which is written concerning us.

14 So Hilkiah the priest, and Ahikam, and Achbor, and Shaphan, and Asahiah, went unto Huldah the prophetess, the wife of Shallum the son of Tikvah, the son of Harhas, keeper of the wardrobe; (now she dwelt in Jerusalem in the college;) and they communed with her.

15 And she said unto them, Thus saith the LORD God of Israel, Tell the man that sent you to me,

16 Thus saith the LORD, Behold, I will bring evil upon this place, and upon the inhabitants thereof,

even all the words of the book which the king of Judah hath read:

17 Because they have forsaken me, and have burned incense unto other gods, that they might provoke me to anger with all the works of their hands; therefore my wrath shall be kindled against this place, and shall not be quenched.

18 But to the king of Judah which sent you to enquire of the LORD, thus shall ye say to him, Thus saith the LORD God of Israel, As touching the words which thou hast heard;

19 Because thine heart was tender, and thou hast humbled thyself before the LORD, when thou heardest what I spake against this place, and against the inhabitants thereof, that they should become a desolation and a curse, and hast rent thy clothes, and wept before me; I also have heard thee, saith the LORD.

20 Behold therefore, I will gather thee unto thy fathers, and thou shalt be gathered into thy grave in peace; and thine eyes shall not see all the evil which I will bring upon this place. And they brought the king word again.

Many women today like the prophetess Huldah are coming forth despite their challenges by many male pastors and have refused to become silent by allowing the enemy to stop their prophetic voices. We must be able to declare the truth of God's Word regardless of gender, be it male or female. Prophetess Huldah was no exception here, she was gifted with prophecy and spoke the Word of God despite a difficult message. Nonetheless, with bravery and faithfulness, she delivered God's warnings. We, too, must speak up and say *"thus says the Lord."* Like prophetess Huldah, you too can have a story that can change your nation's religious consciousness and practises that can ultimately help to turn their love towards God.

CHAPTER 13
THE SPIRIT OF THE EVANGELIST

John 20:18

Mary Magdalene came and told the disciples that she had seen the LORD, and that he had spoken these things unto her.

Friends it is clear here in scripture that, after Mary Magdalene met Jesus at the tomb she ran to share with others, the good news that *"He is risen"*. Here is a true example of an Evangelist carrying such powerful truth; no matter the many disputes by some theologians, it is of truth that He was first seen of by a woman who later revealed to the many others that Jesus was alive, making her the first Evangelist to have spread this powerful truth after the resurrection. Likewise, you and I must also be willing to share the good news of the kingdom, regardless of our gender. We can in no way keep silent when others are in need of us. It's time to sound the alarm by letting the world know that Jesus is very much alive. He is no longer in a tomb, but *He is risen*. Salvation has been handed down, a gift to mankind. There is no silence about our redemptive message. In contrast to this powerful story, there are many others, here is a woman in *John 4:29-30:*

29 *Come, see a man, which told me all things that ever I did: is not this the Christ?*

30 *Then they went out of the city, and came unto him.*

CHAPTER 14
COME SEE A MAN

Here is a true, dynamic story of a woman to whom Jesus had revealed all of her secrets. This woman met Jesus at a well that she was familiar with, as she often went there to draw her water. Little did she know that her hour of Evangelism had come. She later realised the truth of God's Word and as a result became that voice that many desired to hear. She stated, *"come and see a man who tells me all that I have ever done. Is he not the Christ?"* Here this woman's life had been transformed, and she went her way as a powerful Evangelist carrying the true gospel and bringing others to Christ. We likewise can never be quiet after God have opened our eyes to the truth of who He is; it's time we let our lights shine, whether male or female, there is no difference in gender with God.

CHAPTER 15
THE PASTOR
PHEBE GOD'S FAITHFUL SERVANT

Romans 16:1-2

I commend unto you Phebe our sister, which is a servant of the church which is at Cenchrea:

2 That ye receive her in the Lord, as becometh saints, and that ye assist her in whatsoever business she hath need of you: for she hath been a succourer of many, and of myself also.

Here the Apostle Paul makes a perfect description and a good documentary on Pastor Phebe who is God's faithful servant. Even if we are in denial, and want to deny the fact that she is a woman pastor, from the text, these attributes are very clear that Apostle Paul is asking the saints to receive her and to assist her in any area of ministry that she asked of them. Even if you have doubts of her being the first female pastor mentioned, Apostle Paul makes it very clear in this text. Described here in the church her position was not one of a mere thing, her given task was evolving others to work together. It is clear that women don't just sit quiet in the church. God has called each one of us as Paul stated in Ephesians chapter 4: *"he gave some Apostle, Prophetess, Evangelist, Pastors and Teachers."* He didn't say it should be male or female, but he did say that these offices were given to edify and perfect, until the body of Christ became mature. We must never allow the voice of the enemy to silence us from becoming who God has called us to be, we must work the work while it is day, for the night will come when no man is able to work.

CHAPTER 16
THE TEACHER
AQUILA AND PRISCILLA

Acts 18:24-28

24 And a certain Jew named Apollos, born at Alexandria, an eloquent man, and mighty in the scriptures, came to Ephesus.

25 This man was instructed in the way of the Lord; and being fervent in the spirit, he spake and taught diligently the things of the Lord, knowing only the baptism of John.

26 And he began to speak boldly in the synagogue: whom when Aquila and Priscilla had heard, they took him unto them, and expounded unto him the way of God more perfectly.

27 And when he was disposed to pass into Achaia, the brethren wrote, exhorting the disciples to receive him: who, when he was come, helped them much which had believed through grace:

28 For he mightily convinced the Jews, and that publicly, shewing by the scriptures that Jesus was Christ.

Here is a story of a man named Apollos, being born at Alexandria, he was an eloquent man and mighty in scripture. In verse *26* of the above text, he began to speak boldly in the synagogue and *when Aquila and Priscilla had heard, they took him and expounded into him the way of the Lord more perfectly*. Here these two women were great teachers of the Word with a better understanding; they did their very best in helping Apollos to better himself so that he could be more effective. Had these great women teachers remained silent, Apollos would have been somewhat in error as to what he was trying to share in the synagogue at this time. We must never allow the enemy to silence us, it's time to get up and take that stand. Women, you've been destined to win!

CHAPTER 17
LET THE WORD OF GOD SPEAK FOR ITSELF

Jeremiah 31:22

How long wilt thou go about, O thou backsliding daughter? for the Lord hath created a new thing in the earth, A woman shall compass a man.

The scripture here is clear, God has *created a new thing in the Earth, a woman shall compass a man.* It is no doubt that this clause will be disputed, but if you cannot deny the fact that this is not the only time a woman is said to have done such a thing. Here is an example in the book of Judges 4:9, *And she said, I will surely go with thee: notwithstanding the journey that thou takest shall not be for thine honour; for the LORD shall sell Sisera into the hand of a woman. And Deborah arose, and went with Barak to Kedesh.*

Let us take a close look at Barak who God refused to give credit over an enemy army. Why is that so? Because Barak would not go fight them as Israel's sole leader? Without the help of Deborah (his wife) who was accompanied by another woman, finally killed the chief enemy solider Sisera. She was a Jewish lady whose name was Jael. She killed the captain with a tent peg and nailed him straight through the head while he was asleep in her tent. Here it is clear that a woman will do something without a man. We don't have to go very far, take for example the virgin birth, *"behold a virgin shall be with child, and shall bring forth a son, and they shall call his name Emmanuel, which being interpreted is God with us."* Here Joseph had nothing to do with this miracle, when God has destined you and me for a thing, it will surely speak volumes, so that He receives the glory for it.

Matthew 1:20

But while he thought on these things, behold, the angel of the LORD appeared unto him in a dream, saying, Joseph, thou son of David, fear not to take unto thee Mary thy wife: for that which is conceived in her is of the Holy Ghost.

Friends, we must never underestimate the power of a woman with destiny, it goes beyond what the natural eyes can see. Yes, of course you and I have been chosen, and we must be that sound in the Earth that dare to make a difference.

CHAPTER 18
WOMAN OF FAITH
THE SYROPHOENICIAN WOMAN

Matthew 15: 22-28

22 And, behold, a woman of Canaan came out of the same coasts, and cried unto him, saying, Have mercy on me, O Lord, thou son of David; my daughter is grievously vexed with a devil.

23 But he answered her not a word. And his disciples came and besought him, saying, Send her away; for she crieth after us.

24 But he answered and said, I am not sent but unto the lost sheep of the house of Israel.

25 Then came she and worshipped him, saying, Lord, help me.

26 But he answered and said, It is not meet to take the children's bread, and to cast it to dogs.

27 And she said, Truth, Lord: yet the dogs eat of the crumbs which fall from their masters' table.

28 Then Jesus answered and said unto her, O woman, great is thy faith: be it unto thee even as thou wilt.

And her daughter was made whole from that very hour.

Here is a powerful story of a Canaanite woman whose daughter was grievously vexed with a devil. The woman came to Jesus in desperation on behalf of her demon possessed daughter, falling, worshipping at his feet, begging Jesus to help her. Jesus for a few seconds said not a word and his disciples encouraged him to send her way because of continuous torment, but Jesus in return spoke to his disciple saying to them that he had been sent to the lost sheep of Israel. Then came the woman pleading for Jesus' help, but Jesus in return said unto her, *that it was not meant to take the children's bread and cast it to dogs*, referring to the woman as a dog. She stood up in much faith and spoke back, admitting that even dogs eat of the crumbs which fall from their master's table. Jesus in return said unto her, *o woman, great is thy faith: be it unto thee even as thou will, and her daughter was made whole from that very hour.*

Here we can see that this woman was not afraid of challenge despite being called a dog, she was humble and brave enough to speak on behalf of herself and her child. Her unwavering faith and humility has taught us multiple lessons. First, being a Canaanite woman, she was opposite in faith and was contrary in belief when pertaining to God and his Word; it was not lawful to give the children bread to dogs, they were contrary in belief. But nonetheless, she had stepped out of religion to receive what God had for her. We, too, must be willing to let go of religion that makes the gospel of none effect if we are going to be God's voices in the Earth. Here again is the bravery of a woman who was not ashamed to be called names, her persistent determination, strong self will and her unwavering faith had healed her daughter from the torment of demonic interferences. We, too, must be able to step out of the familiar to obtain the blessings of God.

CHAPTER 19
WOMAN OF FAITH
ONE TOUCH

Matthew 9:20-22

20 And, behold, a woman, which was diseased with an issue of blood twelve years, came behind him, and touched the hem of his garment:

21 For she said within herself, If I may but touch his garment, I shall be whole.

22 But Jesus turned him about, and when he saw her, he said, Daughter, be of good comfort; thy faith hath made thee whole. And the woman was made whole from that hour.

Friends, here is a woman who had a blood issue. The Word of God tells us that as a result of this, the woman had spent all that she had seen many different physicians, but her condition only grew worse. Here the Word tells us that she had suffered this problem for twelve long years and was declining daily until she said within herself *if I could only but touch the garment of Jesus*. With so many people enthroning Jesus, to the natural man, this becomes highly impossible, but nonetheless, this woman was persistent in her faith. Her determination had made virtue to leave the body of Jesus; her touch was not just any touch. Her unwavering faith had brought the results of healing to her long term illness. We, too, must have an unwavering faith that is able to move the many mountains out of our lives. We must be that *"If I"*. Never allow the voice of the enemy to silence you.

CHAPTER 20
THE VIRTUOUS WOMAN
WOMAN OF PROMINENCE

Proverbs 31: 10-31

10 Who can find a virtuous woman? for her price is far above rubies.

11 The heart of her husband doth safely trust in her, so that he shall have no need of spoil.

12 She will do him good and not evil all the days of her life.

13 She seeketh wool, and flax, and worketh willingly with her hands.

14 She is like the merchants' ships; she bringeth her food from afar.

15 She riseth also while it is yet night, and giveth meat to her household, and a portion to her maidens.

16 She considereth a field, and buyeth it: with the fruit of her hands she planteth a vineyard.

17 She girdeth her loins with strength, and strengtheneth her arms.

18 She perceiveth that her merchandise is good: her candle goeth not out by night.

19 She layeth her hands to the spindle, and her hands hold the distaff.

20 She stretcheth out her hand to the poor; yea, she reacheth forth her hands to the needy.

21 She is not afraid of the snow for her household: for all her household are clothed with scarlet.

22 She maketh herself coverings of tapestry; her clothing is silk and purple.

23 Her husband is known in the gates, when he sitteth among the elders of the land.

24 She maketh fine linen, and selleth it; and delivereth girdles unto the merchant.

25 Strength and honour are her clothing; and she shall rejoice in time to come.

26 She openeth her mouth with wisdom; and in her tongue is the law of kindness.

27 She looketh well to the ways of her household, and eateth not the bread of idleness.

28 Her children arise up, and call her blessed; her husband also, and he praiseth her.

29 Many daughters have done virtuously, but thou excellest them all.

30 Favour is deceitful, and beauty is vain: but a woman that feareth the LORD, she shall be praised.

31 Give her of the fruit of her hands; and let her own works praise her in the gates.

Here are the words of a wise woman in Proverbs 31:1, the words of King Lemuel and the prophecy that his mother taught him. In this same chapter, verses *10-31* make a signature statement describing a woman of prominence. We don't have to look any further to be able to identify the truth about a virtuous woman. Verses *30* and *31* speak profoundly of her and quotes *"Favour is deceitful, and beauty is vain: but a woman that feareth the LORD, she shall be praised. Give her of the fruit of her hands; and let her own works praise her in the gates."*

Women, you have been chosen to make a difference!

ABOUT THE AUTHOR

Apostle Rosemary Duncanson is a unique and rare vessel to the body of Christ. Apostle Duncanson was born in the Turks and Caicos Islands; she is a mother, Pastor, and Teacher. Having proclaimed the Word of God for more than three decades, her yoke-breaking anointing has helped many  across all spheres of life. Apostle Dunacanson enjoys her outreach ministries and reaches out to as many as possible, calling darkness into light. After many years of pain, hurt, and disappointments, she is proving her ministries entirely and is determined that the enemy will not win. Her determination has given her recognition in every area of her life.

LETTERS TO GOD

WOMEN OF DESTINY

WOMEN OF DESTINY

WOMEN OF DESTINY

WOMEN OF DESTINY

WOMEN OF DESTINY

WOMEN OF DESTINY

WOMEN OF DESTINY